P9-DND-525

COOL
CROSSWORDS
FOR KIDS

By Sam Bellotto Jr.

imagine!
Publishing

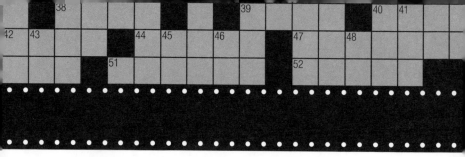

Library of Congress Cataloging-in-Publication Data Available

10 9 8 7 6 5

An Imagine Book
Published by Charlesbridge
85 Main Street
Watertown, MA 02472
617-926-0329
www.charlesbridge.com

Printed in China

ISBN 13: 978-1-936140-88-6

What is the largest animal in the world? How was the mail delivered in the Old West? What can you find in a gym locker? Here are 74 brand-new, never before published crossword puzzles that explore these questions, and much more. They are designed for fun, but they are also full of cool facts about history, geography, science, mathematics, and gooey stuff. They may challenge you, too. That's good. We're sure you are curious about a whole lot of things. It's fine for you to use the Internet and other reference sources to look up and learn all about the clues that stump you. Here's a secret: crosswords for adults have permitted Internet use for years. Just don't ask another person, like your parents, for the answers. There's no fun in that!

Each puzzle has a theme. The longest entries are all about a specific subject, like space travel, or cooking, or bad smells. You can usually figure out the theme from the puzzle's title.

So dig in. We think you will like this collection. We were happy to put it together for you.

ACROSS

1 School rooms for phys ed classes

3 Housefly larva

6 Sights in winter (2 words)

9 Sights in summer (2 words)

12 Sights in autumn (2 words)

16 Sights in spring (2 words)

18 Powerful monkey

19 Biking problem

DOWN

1 Yucky

2 Some iPod downloads

3 Grass cutter

4 Slimy stuff

5 "My country, ___ of thee . . ."

7 Rental agreement

8 Lawn invaders

10 "If ___ knew then what I know now!" (2 words)

11 Blubbered

13 Grass snake's color

14 Stand in art class

15 Cairo is its capital city

16 Sponge___ SquarePants

17 Barbecue meat

ACROSS

1 Neil Armstrong's spacecraft
4 One of the Great Lakes
6 Man-made wonder in China
8 Natural wonder in Arizona
12 Man-made wonder in Paris
17 Man-made wonder in Rome
18 Ache
19 Fall color

DOWN

1 On the way out
2 Substance at the Earth's core
3 Scientist Newton who defined the law of gravity
4 Buzz Aldrin's given name
5 Moray
7 Relaxed
9 Zoo biggie
10 Color one's hair
11 School subject
13 Not a happy face
14 Cowpoke's rope
15 Aunts (but not uncles)
16 Flintlock
17 Bottle top

· THANKSGIVING ·

ACROSS

1 Labrador retriever color
4 One hit Jupiter in 1994
7 Item on a Thanksgiving table
8 Item on a Thanksgiving table
14 Item on a Thanksgiving table
20 Item on a Thanksgiving table
22 Church singers
23 Bellhop's workplace

DOWN

1 Jazz genre
2 Indiana Jones' quest
3 Camera brand
4 Circus performer

5 Florida airport city
6 Norse thunder god with a hammer
9 Mexico's neighbor
10 Baby seal
11 Zambonis make it smooth
12 Letter after upsilon
13 Contact lens spot
15 Baby grand instrument
16 Teen's sign-off
17 Sofa
18 Majestic
19 Gator relative
21 Model maker's purchase

ACROSS

1 Lady's title
4 Broadway star
7 First American woman to go into space (2 words)
8 English novelist who wrote "Pride and Prejudice" (2 words)
13 First person honored with two Nobel Prizes (2 words)
19 Shoshone woman who accompanied Lewis and Clark (2 words)
20 "Shark Tale" jellyfish
21 Jitterbug

DOWN

1 Halloween costume part
2 Greek letter before epsilon
3 Perhaps
4 Good-bye, in French
5 Trick or ___
6 Rat or squirrel
9 "___ won't!" (firm refusal)
10 Circle segment
11 Peppermint Patty, to Marcie
12 ___ State Building
14 Out of bed
15 Game show host
16 Recommended strongly
17 Des Moines resident
18 Weak, as an excuse

ACROSS

1 Rose
4 Largest endangered cat
7 Aircraft that can hover in midair
8 In a funny way
10 Punctuation mark
12 Chess and checkers
15 Fairy tale's last word
17 Hotel booking
18 Grocery carriers
19 Pie-crust crimping areas

DOWN

1 Half the kids in class
2 Lubed
3 Rot
4 Subject of a debate
5 Twinkle
6 Places to eat out
9 Whopper
11 Switch position
13 Class with singing
14 Does a laundry job
15 Out of bed
16 Gadget

ACROSS
1 Dieter's lunch
4 Paperback back
7 Its seeds are a source of cooking oil
8 State flower of Alaska
14 Hummingbirds are attracted to this flower
20 Pond plant where a frog may sit (2 words)
21 Fizzy drinks
22 Klondike locale

DOWN
1 Catch the scent of
2 Buzz Lightyear's weapon
3 Move to the music
4 Oregon capital
5 Cedar Rapids resident
6 Everglades bird
9 Spanish eye
10 "___ whiz!"
11 Third word of "America"
12 PC exit key
13 Hogwarts mail carrier
14 Werewolves wails
15 Celebrated
16 Cookout locales
17 Kwanzaa principle
18 Eskimo canoe
19 Dine at home

· COLORING BOOK ·

ACROSS

1 Short news item
4 Not smooth, as a ride
7 Letters on a postage stamp
8 Long-snouted horse relative
9 Like a cold-sufferer's voice
10 Basketball league abbreviation
11 Long-legged bird of the Everglades
12 Tortilla-chip snack
13 ___ shoestring (frugally)
14 Where wastewater goes
16 "___ ate my homework!"
18 Pie ___ mode (dessert)
19 Devoured
20 Hospital worker
21 Letters between F and J
22 Number of feet in a yard
23 Enlarge the house

DOWN

1 Crayola crayon color since 1949
2 Half of a bunk bed
3 Crayola crayon color since 1954
4 Crayola crayon color since 1997
5 Class with a piano, perhaps
6 Crayola crayon color since 1934
15 Our planet is mostly covered with this
17 Took risks

ACROSS

1 Melting snow
4 Frontiersman Jim at the Alamo
7 Staff member who deals with bullying
8 Faculty member who deals with big numbers
14 Staff member who keeps order
20 Faculty member in charge of everything
21 Where to water camels in the desert
22 Piece of cake

DOWN

1 Bunch of bees
2 In its entirety
3 Ghosts do it
4 Iraq's only seaport
5 Celtic language
6 Mistake
9 Chicken ___ king
10 Evil sci-fi computer in "2001: A Space Odyssey"
11 Conceit
12 Greek X
13 Earth-friendly prefix
14 Second-largest land animal
15 Lions' homes
16 Makes fun of
17 Country where Mount Everest is located
18 Not shutting up
19 Gift for dad

ACROSS

1 Half-human, half-robot
4 Frankenstein's humpbacked helper
6 Enemies of the Autobots
10 One attending school
13 Drink like a dog
14 Chewbacca's friend Solo
15 Exclamation from a greedy person (2 words)
17 "Star Wars" protocol droid, spelled out
21 "Get outta here!"
22 Like peanuts or pretzels

DOWN

1 Fish in a fish sandwich
2 Keyboard key for fixing errors
3 Grammy category for Kanye West
4 Business abbreviation
5 Deteriorating, like an unused robot
7 Rock guitarist Nugent
8 In a difficult or embarrassing position (3 words)
9 Eyewear
11 World Wide Web address
12 Inventor Whitney
16 Feb. follower
18 Square root of four
19 Paleontological period
20 Not even

• FOUR FELINES •

¹		²		³		⁴		⁵		⁶

[Crossword grid with numbered cells: 1, 2, 3, 4, 5, 6 across top row; 7, 8; 9, 10, 11, 12; 13, 14, 15, 16; 17, 18, 19; 20, 21]

ACROSS

1 A cat is said to have nine of them

4 Charlie Parker's jazz genre

7 Big cat species native to the Indian subcontinent (2 words)

9 Town near where the Wright Brothers took their first flight (2 words)

13 Pet that is white with orange and black patches (2 words)

17 Big cat species that lives in Tanzania and Kenya (2 words)

20 Next to last tennis tournament matches

21 Canadian territory noted for gold mining

DOWN

1 Science room

2 Family car

3 Covered with lather

4 Siamese fighting fish

5 "Thanks a ton!" (2 words)

6 Getting an A-plus grade

8 Cotton gin inventor Whitney

9 Residents of the Sunflower State

10 Song syllable

11 Yes, in Japanese

12 Owl's question?

13 Computer disc

14 Secures with a key

15 Halloween giveaway

16 Once upon a time

18 Pen filler

19 Woman in a convent

· STATE BIRDS ·

ACROSS

1 Abduct
4 Neatnik's opposite
6 State bird of Massachusetts
9 State bird of Nebraska
12 State bird of New Mexico
16 State bird of Iowa
19 Measure that is equal to three feet
20 Landing strip

DOWN

1 Boot
2 Roman numeral for 502
3 Percussion instrument

4 Catch a video
5 Three little pigs' house material that could not be blown down
7 Beet with edible leaves
8 Prominent period
10 Hawaiian island noted for pineapples
11 Famous snowman of song
13 Summer month, for short
14 Down ___ (Australia)
15 Part of Miss Muffet's meal
17 Not divisible by two
18 Immediately

ACROSS

1 Canine comment
4 Feet in a yard
6 Spanish gold
7 Refuse (2 words)
8 "Alphabet Song" opening
10 Gold units: Abbreviation
11 Mount climbed by Moses
12 President Wilson's predecessor
13 Lamb's mother
15 "Rise of the Planet of the ___" (2011)
16 Really smells
18 Cable TV channel
19 Postage meter unit
20 Venomous snake
21 Opposite of WSW
22 Power
23 Mattel product

DOWN

1 Lend a hand
2 It'll brown trout (2 words)
3 It'll bake gingerbread men (2 words)
4 It'll cook English muffins (2 words)
5 Genesis garden
9 It'll brew a hot beverage (2 words)
14 Fish-eating hawk
17 Kind of computer virus

ACROSS

1 Fish and ___
4 Smaller replica of an airplane or car
7 Job fixing things
8 Job checking utility usage (2 words)
14 Job hauling products from factory to stores (2 words)
20 Job building homes
21 Sports stadium
22 Sing the Alpine way

DOWN

1 Computer drive
2 Computer data
3 Winter sportsman
4 President Eisenhower's First Lady
5 Had a fancy meal
6 Nonwinner
9 Talent for music
10 Upper-left PC key
11 Color of a boiled lobster
12 "What a good boy ___!" (2 words)
13 Cyclone center
14 Neon aquarium fish
15 Father's brother
16 Land on the Sea of Japan
17 Like some marshes
18 Cast a ballot in an election
19 In the country

ACROSS

1 Possessed
4 Gave a shove
7 Milk "manufacturer"
8 Pleads with
9 What good friends often have
13 You may take this if you're sick
18 World Series month
19 Pothole filler
20 Wood fastener
21 Dieter's lunch order

DOWN

1 Jobs
2 More modern
3 Like 5 Down
4 Top bunk
5 Math class diagram
6 Vanished from sight
10 "Big" circus tent
11 Mr. Potato Head piece
12 Use a sofa
14 Approximately 39 inches
15 Macaroni shape
16 Farmland units
17 Up to now

· TO-DO LIST ·

ACROSS

1 Evening chore
3 Use the bathtub
6 Morning chore (2 words)
8 Hawaiian island
12 Outdoors chore (3 words)
13 Wait at the light
16 Chore involving the family pet (2 words)
18 After dinner chore
19 Fido's feet

DOWN

1 Mayflower ___
2 Leg joint
3 Female
4 Driveway chore (2 words)
5 Grammy category
7 Get out of the way
9 Hits the books
10 Small insect-eater
11 Hands out homework
14 Cut class
15 Family member
17 Web pop-ups

· ON THE MAP ·

ACROSS

1 Country next to Portugal
4 Where Venice is
7 Circle segment
8 Post office purchase
11 Yellow parts of eggs
13 Lima's country
14 Country neighboring Kenya
17 New York and New Jersey
19 Summer month
20 Boise is its capital
22 Some iPod downloads
25 ___ de Janeiro, Brazil
26 Gandhi's land
27 The Pine Tree State

DOWN

1 Titanic's call for help
2 Blind ___ bat
3 Kindergartner's break
4 Like Arctic winds
5 Edgar ___ Poe
6 "Certainly!"
9 Halloween choice
10 Rushmore or St. Helens
12 Second-largest city in Oklahoma
15 Green pear variety
16 New ___ (India capital)
18 Trophy
20 "___ Ran the Circus": Seuss
21 "Are you a good witch ___ bad witch?"
22 She has a day in May
23 Hit the slopes
24 Letters between B and F

ACROSS

1 Miniseries adjective
4 Cheeseburger toppings
7 They can become pickles
8 Fifth grader's age
10 How often pea plants are harvested (2 words)
13 New England cape
14 Button on a camcorder
15 Members of Geronimo's tribe
18 Gridiron official
20 Veggie spear that grows in the spring
21 Veggie growing season
22 Cave sound

DOWN

2 Serve tea
3 Butter maker
4 Path around the sun
5 Where natural pearls come from
6 Popeye's veggie
9 Crunchy snacks for Bugs Bunny
10 Where veggies are grown (3 words)
11 Time period
12 Suffix for yellow
16 Desk mate
17 Hit the delete key
19 Cornmeal dish

· BACK TO SCHOOL ·

ACROSS

1 Pencil-case item
4 It may be prewashed
7 Students carry them
10 The night before a holiday
11 Country that gave us the Statue of Liberty
14 Egyptian god of the afterlife
16 Football filler
18 Classroom necessities
21 Homework assignment
22 Buzz Lightyear's weapon

DOWN

1 What 13 Down is made of
2 Places for schoolbooks

3 Grammy Award category
4 One of the Seven Dwarfs
5 Not yeses
6 Writing on the wall, at times
8 Southwest or Northwest
9 Michael Keaton's role in "Toy Story 3"
12 Waxy drawing items
13 It's on the end of a pencil
15 "How was ___ know?" (2 words)
17 Summer vacation destination
18 Don't do this in class
19 Resurface a road
20 Dance, in French

· SPORTS FANS ·

ACROSS

1 Lawmen at the O.K. Corral
4 Footballs have them
7 Sports arena with service lines and a net (2 words)
8 King Kong was a big one
10 People who hit birdies
13 Indoor sport with pins and alleys
17 Word on a penny
19 Sports arena with touchlines and goalkeepers (2 words)
20 Visits the mall
21 Don't sit

DOWN

1 ___-base hit
2 Where to practice hitting balls
3 What batters do
4 In the neighborhood
5 Slide at a water park
6 Places on the Internet
9 Some amateur athletes turn this
11 Dominate, in sports talk
12 Baseball score
13 There are four on a baseball field
14 Crazy
15 Deep thinkers get them
16 Birthday presents
17 Classical music drama
18 Shut down

· BUGGY ·

ACROSS

1 Where some people keep crickets
4 Pet lizard
7 Florida city or river
8 Cobwebby area
9 "A Bug's Life" princess
10 One of the senses
11 Address for a fictional fox
12 Computer memory
14 Aslan of Narnia
15 Giant insect from outer space
17 Number of legs on a crayfish
18 E-mail option
19 Spills the beans
20 Say "yes"
21 Does a laundry job

DOWN

1 Snowball in space
2 Leaping insect
3 Arachnid
4 Tiny summer pest
5 Insect that spins a cocoon
6 "Sesame Street" grouch
13 Praying insect
14 Baby bug
16 Hornet homes
17 Use a keyboard

ACROSS

1 Intricate
7 Homer Simpson's sister-in-law
8 Sports stadium
9 Round Table title
10 Cinnamon, for example
11 Oliver of fiction
12 Complete a crossword
14 Ice-cream measures
16 Toothpaste type
17 Poet Dickinson
18 Lewis Carroll heroine
19 Not heavy

DOWN

1 Prices
2 Working a "times" problem in math class
3 Renter's contract
4 Reading at the optician's
5 Disney movie with Simba, Nala, and Scar
6 Rough sketch
12 Fish market feature
13 Pyramids of Giza locale
14 Baseball pitcher's target
15 Sugarcoated

• DINO DELIGHT •

ACROSS
1 Piece of pizza
4 Like some "Jurassic Park" scenes
7 Three-horned dinosaur
11 Actor Wylie or Sandler
12 Jack Sparrow is one
15 Dinosaur hunter's find
18 Clothing department
19 King of the dinosaurs
24 Finish all of one's dinner (2 words)
25 Gravy shouldn't be this

DOWN
1 Command to a dog
2 "___ Ran the Zoo" by Dr. Seuss (2 words)
3 Day before a holiday
4 "Finding Nemo" setting
5 Good smell
6 "Okay!"
8 XM Satellite ___
9 Hair straighteners
10 Musical talk
13 You wear these over pajamas
14 "Happy Birthday ___!" (2 words)
16 Jack in nursery rhymes who ate no fat
17 Letters between K and O
19 Sneaker part
20 Letters between M and Q
21 Hooting bird
22 Where to get a flu shot
23 Cowboy Rogers who rode Trigger

ACROSS

1 Curly punctuation mark
4 Alexander Graham Bell invention
7 Spider-Man, for one
9 James Bond, for one
14 What 7 Across, 9 Across, and 19 Across do
19 Sherlock Holmes, for one
21 Largest animal in the world
22 Wicked

DOWN

1 What 19 Across looks for
2 Contents of some CDs
3 Pie fruit
4 Winter coat
5 Word on a penny
6 Environmental prefix
8 Kitchen stove
10 Eat away at
11 Race the engine
12 Tic-___-toe
13 Between F and J
15 Variety show host
16 Sit on the throne
17 Some competitions
18 Like insect guts
19 Moisture on the lawn
20 Hot or iced drink

ACROSS

1 Celebrated
3 Part of a bicycle
7 Guitarist's gadget
8 A reptile
9 Hip-hop's ___ Kim
10 "Harry Potter" monster
12 Home for an Eskimo
14 Giuseppi Verdi musical work
15 Old Testament twin
17 Chinese restaurant drink
18 Part of a makeover
19 Schoolbook
20 Shrek's color
21 Anaconda or boa

DOWN

1 Lizards with suction-cup feet
2 Kind of chameleon
4 Winged fire breathers of fables
5 Ambassador's wife
6 Large swamp-dwelling reptile
11 Dinosaur, for example
13 Loggerhead or leatherback
15 No longer on the plate
16 Thick carpet

ACROSS

1 Civil War general who became president

4 President who annexed Texas

6 President who defeated George Bush and Bob Dole (2 words)

9 Doofus

12 Put into practice

13 Grown-up

14 Thingamajigs

17 He became president after Franklin Roosevelt died (2 words)

20 Second president of the United States

21 President who resigned from office

DOWN

2 Everybody

3 ___-tac-toe

4 Like a pigtail

5 Salad ingredient

6 Wicked

7 Fuel for the fireplace

8 Opposite of SSW

10 West African country next to Chad

11 Owls stare with them (2 words)

13 Word from Ebenezer Scrooge

15 Zoo animal

16 Father's Day giver

18 Do a marathon

19 Blend

· WATERLOGGED ·

ACROSS

1 Nightmare
4 Polish
7 World's largest island
9 Japan's second largest island
13 Australian island and state
17 Oldest and most densely populated New York City island
20 Mashed potatoes go-with
21 Toothsome

DOWN

1 Man's best friend
2 Gaze
3 Chutney ingredient
4 Predator of the deep
5 Bicycle spokes
6 Baggins in "The Hobbit"
8 Cuban dance
9 ___ on rye
10 Relatives
11 Small battery size
12 Pulitzer Prize category
13 Creature
14 Its capital is Apia
15 Pester
16 Vatican City's country
18 Male turkey
19 Congressional "no"

ACROSS

1 Theater employee
4 Mountain feature
7 Natural bathtub (2 words)
9 Local theater from June to September (2 words)
14 Olympics featuring skiing and bobsledding (2 words)
19 Niagara has a famous one
21 Like hip-hop pants
22 Gridiron measures

DOWN

1 Computer buffs
2 Boring
3 Tighten sneakers

4 Lassoes
5 Roman numeral 601
6 It's cracked in the kitchen
8 Cubbyhole
10 Seat of Oneida County, New York
11 Gym pad
12 Robotic play by Karel Capek
13 Coffee alternative
15 Ahead of time
16 Thanksgiving sauce
17 Back tooth
18 Luncheon choices
19 Internet area
20 Schoolyard game

ACROSS

1 Tree covering
3 Hay-fever symptom
7 She'll treat a classroom injury (2 words)
11 Prefix for bike
12 Internet room
14 Like parents or teachers
15 Young deer
17 Reverse
18 This can keep you from getting sick
22 Mother Goose poems
23 Road emergency

DOWN

1 School vehicle
2 Cheer
4 Opposite of "Oui!"
5 Planet that we live on
6 Circumstance
8 Yangtze River country
9 Hot-dog topping
10 Take a nap (2 words)
12 Pizza leftover
13 TV-menu heading
15 Flu symptom
16 Crazy
19 Hockey rink
20 Sick
21 Granola ingredient

ACROSS

1 Old King Cole's request
4 Zoo animals
7 Hans Christian Andersen tale about a tiny girl
8 Girl in a tale of a house where 14 Across live
14 Papa, mama, and baby in a tale with 8 Across
19 Tale also known as "The Little Glass Slipper"
20 Sings Swiss-style
21 Rouse from sleep

DOWN

2 Dog collar attachment

3 Identical, in math class
4 Synagogue leader
5 Eskimo home
6 Not abundant
9 Move a rowboat with this
10 Deer mom
11 Civil War losing general
12 Lightning McQueen or Tow Mater
13 Gooey
15 Actor Murphy in "Shrek"
16 Kennel sounds
17 Permit
18 Great white of the ocean

· MUSIC MAKERS ·

ACROSS

1 Gem found in an oyster
4 Alligator's home
7 Kind of music for which there is no description
8 Kind of music popularized by Elvis Presley (3 words)
13 Kind of music written by Mozart
18 Kind of folk music that has been around for centuries
19 Brother's daughter
20 White-plumed wading bird

DOWN

1 Frisbee material

2 TV show performer
3 Song words
4 Madrid is this country's capital
5 Friend in 4 Down
6 Boston cream ___
9 Approves
10 Colorful carp
11 Compact-disc inventor
12 Flier
14 Astound
15 Icky goo
16 Batman fights it
17 Moon-related
18 Sunbathe

· BORROWED ·

ACROSS

1 Person from India who celebrates Diwali

4 School supply

7 Borrow this to inflate a flat tire (2 words)

8 What a girl may borrow because she has nothing to wear to school (2 words)

14 Borrow this from your parents, maybe (2 words)

21 Borrow this for a reading assignment (2 words)

22 Capital and largest city in Belarus

23 Really stinks

DOWN

1 Freight train hoppers

2 Vampire's targets

3 What to call your mom's brother

4 Push forward

5 Mickey Mouse's dog

6 Like a ready-to-eat banana

9 Sick

10 Fifth grader's age

11 Cheer from the bleachers

12 Square root of four

13 Pumpkin ___

15 Metropolitan

16 Blackboard marker

17 Top elected official of a city

18 Lasso loop

19 Harnesses for oxen

20 Chowder ingredient

· EARLY START ·

ACROSS

1 Computer lists of options
4 ___ stomach (needs antacid)
7 First thing to do in the morning (3 words)
8 Second thing to do in the morning (3 words)
13 Third thing to do in the morning (2 words)
18 Fourth thing to do in the morning (3 words)
20 Striped big cat
21 Sign on a front door

DOWN

1 School subject
2 Big brand of smartphones

3 One of 50 on a US map
4 "Yep!"
5 Use a needle and thread
6 Ready for bed
8 Soccer star Hamm
9 Keystone ___ of old silent movies
10 Peak
11 Chapter in history
12 "The Lord of the Rings" creature
13 Disney theme park in Orlando, Florida
14 Turn the ___ cheek
15 Make of Chevy SUV
16 Mechanical man
17 Old Russian ruler
19 Schoolyard game

ACROSS

1 Computer problem
4 One of the Chipmunks
7 Some music or videos from the Internet
9 Small data storage device with a USB port (2 words)
13 Use this to text, take pictures, or play games
17 Device for watching movies on disc (2 words)
20 Ice cream serving
21 It hooks the computer to the Internet

DOWN

1 ___ President

2 Fishing pole
3 Embroider
4 Neither liquid nor gaseous
5 Florida city on Biscayne Bay
6 More curious, maybe
8 Doing a live radio show (2 words)
10 Bunny bounce
11 River of France
12 Whispered comments
14 Part of a TV signal
15 Flower from the Netherlands
16 Nightcrawler
18 Thanksgiving veggie
19 Stop sign color

· LOOKING UP ·

ACROSS

1 Shower-curtain holders
4 Vishnu worshipper
7 Practical and realistic
8 Neil Armstrong was the first on 7/21/1969
12 Symbols of Kansas
16 Meteor, slangily
18 Places for sprinklers
19 "Teenage Mutant ___ Turtles"

DOWN

1 Unmannerly
2 Infant
3 Glossy fabric
4 Laughing scavenger
5 Neither here ___ there
6 Guides with flashlights
9 Owl's question?
10 Stuff of nails and scales
11 Utile
13 Dragon dens
14 Roomy car
15 District
17 Regulation

• SHIVER ME TIMBERS •

ACROSS

1 ___ Road ice cream
4 Part of a BLT sandwich
7 Peter Pan's archenemy
   (2 words)
8 The Black Pearl is one
   (2 words)
12 Skull and crossbones flag
   flown by 8 Across
   (2 words)
16 This can help a pirate find
   a buried chest (2 words)
18 An 8 Across has at least
   two
19 Plants have them

DOWN

1 Cooking directions
2 Baseball uniform part
3 It causes dough to rise
4 Skeleton parts
5 In the oven
6 Sneaker brand
9 People engaged in civil
   unrest
10 Cambridge cathedral city
11 Sources of raisins
13 Comes in second
14 More difficult to find
15 Part of a molecule
17 Cow call

· WHAT'S FOR DINNER ·

ACROSS

1 Laughable
4 Thighbone
7 Fast-food order (2 words)
8 Dinner with meatballs
13 Picnic dinner (2 words)
19 Dinner at a seafood restaurant (2 words)
20 Caveman's weapon
21 Indoor target game

DOWN

1 Coffeehouse
2 Track events
3 Chocolate drink
4 Elementary school grade
5 Slightly wet
6 Moscow is its capital
9 Playmate
10 "In ___ We Trust" (US motto)
11 Breakfast food
12 Mars a shoeshine
14 "Who's there?" reply
15 "You're ___ a surprise!"
16 Lubricated
17 Take an oath
18 Seeks answers

· I WONDER ·

ACROSS

1 First word of a question
4 Civil War soldier from the South
7 More of a question (3 words)
8 Positive response
11 Mother chicken
12 More of a question (2 words)
13 Common name for a lion
14 Summon a genie
16 End of a question (3 words)
19 Opponents of 4 Across
20 Middle of three ear bones

DOWN

1 Pooped
2 Internet address
3 Number 10 ___ Street (British Prime Minister's home)
4 Mouse relative
5 Family member
6 Language of ancient Rome
9 Puffed up
10 Destructive tidal wave
13 ___ rabbit's foot
15 Tour de France vehicles
17 UFO pilots
18 Circle segment

ACROSS

1 What a paper airplane does
4 Largest continent
6 Courageous
8 Sweater type
11 Street smarts
16 Small change
17 "___ in Boots" (2011 movie)
18 Range

DOWN

1 Fort Knox content
2 Inexpensive eatery
3 Aroma
4 Kitchen wear
5 Put two and two together
7 TV gameshow host
8 A dentist may drill into one
9 Little piggy
10 Cyclops feature
12 Foot warmers
13 Stockholm citizen
14 "Jack Sprat could eat ___ . . ."
15 Word on a word processor menu
16 Policeman

ACROSS

1 Three-dimensional
4 Heavenly harpist
7 Animal performers under the Big Top
9 Get older
10 Fearless performer under the Big Top
15 Whip-holding performer under the Big Top (2 words)
20 Item on a concert stage
21 Muscular performer under the Big Top (2 words)
23 Chew loudly
24 Word on a yellow traffic sign

DOWN

1 Coating for popcorn or apples
2 Need a bandage
3 Nice weather forecast
4 Was sore
5 Squirt ___
6 What the L in LA stands for
8 Prefix meaning three
11 Raggedy ___ (doll)
12 Government group that enforces the Clean Air Act: Abbreviation
13 A cyclops has only one
14 Spotted African cat
16 Suffix for violin
17 ___ grade (high school class)
18 Halloween costume
19 Kitchen appliance
21 US uncle
22 Hurry

• READING MATERIAL •

ACROSS

1 Was in a marathon
4 Parts of speech
7 It might be read in homeroom (2 words)
8 They might be read outside of classes (2 words)
13 It might be read at home (2 words)
18 It might be read in classes (2 words)
20 School employee
21 Author of Sherlock Holmes stories

DOWN

1 Bad-mannered
2 Winter warmer-upper
3 Slobber
4 Hasta la ___
5 Brazil resort city
6 Footprints
8 Dirt chopper
9 Zodiac lion
10 Rainbow's end
11 "Shark Tale" setting
12 Cut short
13 Varnish ingredient
14 ___ Island (state)
15 Valentine's Day figure
16 Answer
17 Costing nothing
19 Him counterpart

ACROSS

1 Class competition (2 words)
7 Gusts of wind
8 Loosen laces
9 Weight for bricks
10 Orchestral section
11 Sugarcoated
12 Give private lessons
14 ___ Duck of cartoons
16 Environmentally friendly
17 Downgrade
18 Civil War side
19 Symbols (shown here) used in math and English

DOWN

1 ___ Mario Bros.
2 Tourist attraction in Paris (2 words)
3 Shoppers' aids
4 Adjectives modify them
5 Insects that start out as caterpillars
6 Vote into office
12 Flower from the Netherlands
13 Broadcast on TV again
14 You knead this to make bread
15 Extracts a tooth

• GREAT BOOKS •

ACROSS

1 Bunch of bees
4 Bursts of wind
7 "The Adventures of ___" by Mark Twain (2 words)
9 Book by Charles Dickens (2 words)
14 Book by American author Louisa May Alcott (2 words)
18 Fantasy novel by J. R. R. Tolkien (2 words)
21 Tattered and torn
22 Where the deer and the antelope play

DOWN

1 It's over your head
2 School subject
3 President Eisenhower's wife
4 Beanstalk biggie
5 "Heidi" author
6 "Jack ___ could eat no . . ."
8 "___ want for Christmas . . ." (2 words)
10 Dog doctor
11 Ham sandwich bread
12 "Which one?"
13 Snowbank slider
14 In the future
15 Halloween choice
16 Crazy
17 "Euryanthe" composer Carl Maria von ___
19 Square root of 100
20 Nursery "piggy"

ACROSS

1 Desert over half of Israel
4 Fuss in front of the mirror
7 Where to screw in an incandescent bulb (2 words)
8 Jewelry worn around a girl's neck (2 words)
13 Vehicle that can go to the moon (2 words)
17 Old-fashioned timepiece (2 words)
20 Delicious
21 Nursery ___

DOWN

1 Longest river in the world
2 Choke
3 Cast a ballot
4 Snapshot
5 Ballpoint contents
6 It may be French-fried
9 "The Lord of the Rings" monster
10 On fire
11 Colorful fish in a backyard pond
12 Award
14 Joker, to Batman
15 Waste carrier under the streets
16 Roller coaster shout
18 Web-video gear
19 Attempt

ACROSS

1 Camels have them
4 Cut like a deli sandwich (2 words)
7 Topping for 14 Across
8 SpongeBob's squirrel friend from Texas (2 words)
14 Fast food item made by SpongeBob (2 words)
19 SpongeBob's next-door neighbor and coworker
21 Pool marking
22 Like a boat with holes in it

DOWN

1 Letters after G
2 Cantaloupe
3 Shrewdly
4 People who celebrate St. Patrick's Day
5 Nevada resort near Carson City
6 Stinks
9 What you breathe
10 Small amount
11 Weep
12 Historic time
13 Young beaver
14 Work dough
15 Ancient Greek teller of many fables
16 Painter's need
17 Bike part
18 Miss America's crown
20 Towel off

• THINGS THAT FLY •

ACROSS

1 Devoted
4 Text a short message
7 They're handmade by folding a page from a tablet (2 words)
9 Aircraft also known as a whirlybird
14 It's blown out of a toy pipe (2 words)
19 They fly south for the winter in vee formations (2 words)
22 Mucky
23 "Robinson Crusoe" author

DOWN

1 Drink like a dog
2 Talk foolishly
3 Song words
4 Flower from Holland
5 One of a Muppet duo
6 Midterm
8 Geometry calculations
10 "___ little teapot . . ."
11 Round figure
12 Where a rubber ducky swims
13 Regulations to follow
15 Possessed
16 Chunky
17 Strongly suggested
18 Dirty water coating
20 Keebler baker
21 Place for a patch

• MATH PROBLEMS •

ACROSS

1 It travels at approximately 186,282 miles per second

4 Martin Luther King had one

7 How many centimeters in 4 meters (spelled out)?

9 What is the square root of 441 (spelled out)?

14 What is 21 x 3 + 6 (spelled out)?

19 What is 9/30 in its lowest terms (spelled out)?

21 Dried dishes

22 Tall and thin

DOWN

1 Towering

2 Sound like a pig

3 Lake near Carson City, Nevada

4 Jelly ___

5 Rabbit feature

6 Hatter of Wonderland

8 Volcano in Sicily

10 Soaked

11 Opposite of "oui" in French

12 Japanese coin

13 Use a rod and reel

15 Surrender

16 Standard of perfection

17 Wolfed down

18 Homework assignment

19 Pull a waterskier

20 Kanye West's music

ACROSS

1 Handlebar covers
4 One of Santa's reindeer
7 City employee with a badge
9 School employee with a calculator (2 words)
14 Delivery company employee with a road map (2 words)
19 NASA employee with a space suit
21 Eskimo canoe
22 One of the Great Lakes

DOWN

1 Sparkle

2 Computer fodder
3 Sound of a falling tomato
4 Drink with marshmallows
5 Family member
6 Element with an atomic number of 50
8 Keep ___ on (watch over)
10 Farm units
11 Ad ___ committee
12 Conclude
13 22nd Greek letter
15 Door sound
16 Household pest
17 Election Day participant
18 Wisconsin's state bird
19 Question
20 Playpen item

ACROSS

1 Italian restaurant favorite
4 Popular pie with pepperoni
7 Heroine from the "Terminator" movies (2 words)
9 Hero from Sherwood Forest (2 words)
13 Hero from the British Secret Service (2 words)
17 Hero from Hogwarts School (2 words)
20 TV repeat
21 Bronze place

DOWN

1 Battery terminal: Abbreviation
2 Round Table title
3 Colorless
4 Glossy
5 Like a soccer field
6 Ditsy one
8 Long time ___
9 Livestock owner
10 Tax-deferred savings account: Abbreviation
11 Tint
12 Sphere
13 Panel member
14 Guatemalan native
15 Teakettle feature
16 Opposite of SSW
18 Angular prefix
19 Stoplight color

· FOR BREAKFAST ·

ACROSS

1 Breakfast food
4 State tree of Texas
7 Breakfast food (2 words)
10 Antlered animal
11 Breakfast food
14 Breakfast food
16 Hockey-stick wood
18 Breakfast drink
22 Breakfast food
23 Aladdin's lamp inhabitant

DOWN

1 Little shepherdess who lost her sheep
2 Cereal sound
3 "Forget it!"
4 Group of whales
5 Machine part
6 Pinocchio's lie detector
8 Teach
9 North Pole worker
12 Language of Rome
13 Pizza topping
15 Jog
17 Farm animal with horns
19 Chicken ___ king
20 Stomach
21 Large bottle

```
 1 |   | 2 |   | 3 |███| 4 |   | 5 |   | 6
   |███|   |███|   |███|   |███|   |███|
 7 |   |   |   |   |   |   |   |   |   |
   |███|   |███|   |███|███|███|   |███|
 8 | 9 |   |███|10 |   |11 |   |███|12 |
███|   |███|███|   |███|   |███|███|███|
13 |14 |   |   |   |   |   |███|15 |   |16
   |███|   |███|███|   |   |███|   |███|
17 |   |   |   |18 |   |   |   |   |   |
   |███|   |███|   |███|   |███|   |███|
19 |   |   |   |   |███|20 |   |   |   |
```

ACROSS

1 Address for a woman president

4 ". . . ___ waves of grain"

7 SpongeBob ___

8 Hatted Seuss character

10 Like 7 Across or 16 Down

13 Disney character with an English stepbrother named Ferb

15 Summit

17 Where to find 7 Across on TV

19 Floor

20 Give it that ___ effort

DOWN

1 Country or classical

2 Question

3 Wonder

4 Serpent of the Nile

5 It's picked in Nashville

6 Evergreen goop

9 Pompeii fallout

11 Freshen

12 Tic-tac-toe winner

13 Game-show group

14 Suffering from poison ivy

15 Text a short message

16 Kung Fu ___

18 Audience

· WELL STATED ·

ACROSS
1 Its capital is Carson City
4 Route through a mountain range
6 State where Coca-Cola was first bottled
8 Command to Fido
10 One of the 13 original colonies
13 Everglades state
15 Souvenir of Hawaii
17 State that grows the most sunflowers
18 Computer recording medium
19 New ___ (the Garden State)

DOWN
1 Identifies
2 Go and see
3 At work on
4 Gripping tool
5 Kind of lodge at Aspen
7 Cost
9 Eskimo abode
11 Finish
12 Alaska's circle
14 Not sleeping
15 Big cats from Kenya
16 Country near France
17 Head movement

ACROSS

1 Lobster eater's wear
3 Cocker ___ (sporting dog)
7 Short wire-haired dog with a beard
9 Spy device
10 "Wiener dog"
14 Labrador ___ (bird dog)
17 Beam of sunshine
18 Like the zebra
20 Boston terrier's kin
21 Ham sandwich bread

DOWN

1 Next to

2 Buckaroo bucker
3 Command to Fido
4 Data from tree rings
5 Sleeping
6 A dog has four
8 Acquire the family fortune, perhaps
11 Garden tool
12 Opposite of SSW
13 Overpass
14 Majestic
15 Poisonous snake
16 Seafood buffet choice
18 Singing the blues
19 Scott Joplin tune

· JUST DESSERTS ·

ACROSS

1 Harry Potter's specialty
4 Room at the top of the house
7 Fruit-filled dessert
9 Took a chair
10 Popular ice cream flavor
14 Kind of muffin
18 Sound from a cow
19 Strawberry ___
22 Dough ingredient
23 Cowboy's ride

DOWN

1 Short name for a common apple
2 Seventh letter
3 Freighter contents
4 First Greek letter
5 Answer to "Which ones?"
6 Pie filling, made with eggs
8 Triumphant exclamation
10 Like brownies
11 Pigeon sound
12 Letters between K and O
13 Pothole filler
14 ___ Rica, Central America
15 Henhouse perch
16 Big bunch of cookies
17 Inquire
20 Atmosphere
21 Contact lens spot

ACROSS

1 Toss waste paper here
4 Product on a tub ledge, maybe
6 Bathroom item that comes in rolls (2 words)
8 Pajama halves
10 Play miniature golf
12 Latin-American dance
13 Clothes off
15 Black-and-white killer whale
17 It may be hot or cold in the bathroom (2 words)
19 Sleeping quarters?
20 Dressing-table feature

DOWN

1 Place for a soak or a shower
2 Pinch pennies
3 Contact lens location
4 Hair-care product
5 Secret ___
7 Stop using the TV or computer (2 words)
9 Supreme Court justice John Paul ___
11 Kitchen appliance
14 Out of bed
16 Lightweight bike
18 Prince in "Aladdin"

• WORD WEB 3 •

1
2
3
4
5
6
7
8
9
10
11
12
13
14
15
16
17
18
19

ACROSS

1 Backyard barbecue site
4 Protection for Sir Lancelot
7 Resident of San Francisco or Los Angeles
8 Hammerhead's home
9 Roman numeral 300
10 Boot part
11 Gardening tool
12 Birthday question
13 Organization with 19 Acrosses
14 Concealed
15 Pester
17 Commotion
18 High schoolers
19 Spy

DOWN

1 Eats like a chicken
2 Capital city of Florida
3 Times that the doctor is available
4 Magical word
5 What a school janitor does
6 Cowboy's stamping ground
13 Starfleet Academy student
16 ___ white shark

ACROSS

1 Dark ___
3 Keeper of the Keys and Grounds Hagrid
6 "The boy who lived"
9 Source of music
10 Fred and George Weasley created a portable one
13 One of Hogwarts' founders and creator of Hufflepuff House
15 Like 3 Across
17 He escaped Azkaban prison
20 Death ___ (Lord Voldemort's followers)
21 Where a pet door leads to often

DOWN

1 Campfire residue
2 The ___ Hat
3 It may be skipped
4 Magical Menagerie offering
5 Throw out
7 Fill with wonder
8 Colonial taxed item
11 Family name at Ottery St. Catchpole, Devon
12 Professor Binns teaches its history
13 Hurry-scurry
14 Roman household god
16 Seeks answers
18 Windshield scraper's scrapings
19 Grade-schooler

· WILD WEST ·

ACROSS
1 Cowboy contests
4 Important party
6 Outlaws or lawmen of the Old West
8 Tyrannosaurus ___
9 Loop under a saddle
12 Masked men of the Old West
15 Use a hammock
17 Postal service of the Old West
19 ". . . where the ___ and the antelope play"
20 Cowboy's seat

DOWN
1 Jolly ___ (pirate flag)
2 Santa's helper
3 Marksman's aid
4 Everglades critter
5 Fable teller of old
7 Eisenhower's vice president
9 Chem. or biol.
10 Smartness stats
11 Cowboy's stamping ground
12 Two-footed animal
13 Hair-styling tool
14 Where the Alamo is remembered
16 Sheriff's band
18 Clown nose color

ACROSS

1 Popular programming language
4 Roadside warning light
7 Computer storage device
11 Tech trip to fix a broken PC
14 Computer program
16 Used the inkjet again
21 Land of pyramids
22 Computer peripheral

DOWN

1 "Humbug!"
2 Term of respect
3 Fish-stick fish
4 It follows 19 Down
5 Concert venue
6 Computer messages
8 Licked the platter clean
9 Beelzebub
10 Speedway speeder
12 Interrupt
13 Out of the box, perhaps
14 Maker of the iMac or iPod
15 Birthday event
17 Big belly
18 Dr. Seuss' Sam ___
19 Wed. follower
20 Color eggs

ACROSS

1 Some have bubbles
4 Coffeehouse order
7 Items used in geography class (2 words)
8 Items used in art class (2 words)
13 Item used in math class
18 Items used in science class
20 President Obama's youngest daughter
21 It can be obtuse or acute

DOWN

1 Eat cereal out of it
2 Road goo
3 Winner of the Nobel Peace Prize in 1978
4 Garden material
5 Hooded snake
6 Help out
9 Computer key
10 Silicon Valley's state: Abbreviation
11 Kitchenware item
12 Pranksters
14 Doggy kisses
15 "Once ___ time . . ."
16 Capital city of Ghana
17 Small island
19 Squealer

ACROSS

1 Dog on "The Jetsons"
4 Batman's partner
7 Disney/Pixar movie about a lost fish
9 Neglect
11 Adams of "Get Smart"
13 Summon a genie
15 Animated movie with a mammoth
18 Feature cartoon starring Simba, Scar, and Nala
20 Heroine of "The Princess and the Frog"
21 Murphy in Shrek movies

DOWN

1 Bruce Wayne's butler
2 Friend of Snowy and Captain Haddock
3 Hamburger topper
4 Rabbit of Toontown
5 Jerry Seinfeld cartoon role
6 Keanu Reeve's role in "The Matrix"
8 Computer command list
10 Word on a penny
12 Response to a pinprick
13 Put away a garden hose
14 Long-eared hound
16 "Kung Fu Panda" country
17 Musical based on a little orphan of comics
18 Part of a drumbeat
19 Chapter in history

· PARTY TIME ·

ACROSS

1 What a relative might send for 19 Across

4 Place to hide gifts

6 Time off from school

8 Opposite of don'ts

10 Party food (2 words)

12 Pigeon sound

13 Suffix for guitar

14 When many parties are held

17 Whitney who invented the cotton gin

19 Occasion when candles are lit

20 ___ numeral (like IV or X)

21 Planet with a 365-day orbit

DOWN

2 Lunch-box cookie

3 It causes dough to rise

4 San Antonio landmark

5 Colorful paper thrown during festivals

7 Place for a rainy day party

8 When to have a New Year's Eve party

9 Party for a bride-to-be

11 N. or S. state

15 Patriot Allen of 1776

16 Clear the blackboard

18 Like Bo Peep's sheep

• WEATHER REPORT •

ACROSS

1 Monarchs
4 Source of rain
7 Rain with ice pellets
11 Monkey in Disney's "Aladdin"
13 Colorful arc after the rain
15 Cause of a day off from school
16 Deli bread
18 Violent winds
22 Like a summer day
23 Nairobi locale

DOWN

1 Australian marsupial
2 India's first prime minister
3 Compete in super G
4 Computer inserts
5 Tic-tac-toe row
6 Beaver construction
8 Comprehended
9 Microscopic
10 Like a luxury car
12 Bluegrass instrument
14 Graceful bird
16 Out of bed
17 Give it that ___ effort
18 Some are high-definition
19 Baseball score
20 ". . . have you ___ wool?"
21 Acorn source

1		2		3		4		5		6
						7				
8							9		10	
11	12		13			14		15		16
17		18		19						
20										
				21						

ACROSS

1 New England vacation area

7 View from San Francisco

8 Oldest US national park

11 Scandinavian language

14 Storage room for an old trunk

17 Wonder of the Natural World in Arizona

20 Mouse pointer on a computer

21 Famous falls near Buffalo, NY

DOWN

1 Coloring book need

2 Fast-growing tree with circular leaves

3 Prairie predator

4 Boxers and spaniels

5 "Finding ___" (2003)

6 First word of a fairy tale

9 Egyptian boy king

10 In first place, for short

12 Rowboat rower

13 Solar system center

14 Mount McKinley locale

15 Japanese car model

16 Ottawa is its capital

17 Soccer score

18 Unit of farm land

19 Early light

• DATE LINES •

ACROSS

1 Seize

4 Computer button that turns it on

7 Celebrated as the start of summer

8 Holiday celebrating the birth of the USA

13 ___ Day (February 14)

18 Time to ring out the old and ring in the new

20 Ahead of schedule

21 Disney's flying elephant

DOWN

1 Checkers or chess

2 Triceps location

3 Petunia Pig's love

4 Alicia Keys' instrument

5 Dentist's request

6 Tempo

9 Wranglers' rival

10 Overweight

11 Coffeepot with a spigot

12 Boulevard

14 Bottom bunk

15 Poverty-stricken

16 How mistakes are marked

17 Worst grade

19 Hardwood tree

ACROSS

1 Starfleet Academy student
4 Questionable
7 Results of some playground accidents
9 Cat owners change this often
14 Plant that can give you an itchy rash
19 Items in a gym locker
21 Neither liquid nor gaseous
22 Pyramids of Giza locale

DOWN

1 Ice shapes
2 Hungry dog slobber
3 Send a short text message
4 Aesop's story
5 Junior
6 Survey choice
8 Where Prince Harry of England went to college
10 Cards with personal info
11 Bart Simpson's age
12 Gun the engine
13 Early bird's reward
15 Lubricated
16 Magazine copy
17 Word to describe 19 Across or 2 Down
18 House call
19 Oceanic "help!"
20 Sushi dish

· TOP DOGS ·

ACROSS
1 Canine sound
3 Metropolis paper, for short
8 Tiny dog from Mexico
9 Short-legged hunting dog (2 words)
15 Reddish-brown sporting dog (2 words)
21 Scooby-Doo's dog breed (2 words)
22 Tune
23 Puppy's dinner

DOWN
1 Book jacket writing
2 Some are sedimentary

4 Be in stitches
5 First prime minister of India
6 Orange pekoe
7 Cursor clickers
10 Atmosphere
11 Last message of the Titanic
12 Cable "Superstation"
13 Pick
14 Opposite of SSW
16 Perfection
17 Detested
18 Semester tester
19 Molars
20 Extend a subscription
21 Goo on a shoe

ACROSS

1 Sun blocker
4 Schoolroom supply
7 Gift for sister (2 words)
8 Gift for younger sister (2 words)
12 Gift for younger brother (2 words)
16 Gift for brother (2 words)
18 Description for a haunted house
19 ___-cured ham

DOWN

1 Price
2 Squeak remedy
3 Dork
4 Secret supply
5 One way to order pie
6 Tenderly
9 Capital city of Maine
10 Real-time AOL exchanges
11 Geography class fixtures
13 Domestic cat
14 Reference book with maps
15 Lucky Charms charm
17 Insect

• SMELLS AWFUL •

ACROSS
1 Leaps
4 Uses a paper towel
7 Excellent fertilizer that smells awful (2 words)
8 It smells awful if you don't flush it (2 words)
13 After gym class, they can smell awful (2 words)
19 It smells awful washed up on the beach (2 words)
20 Largest marine mammal
21 Book name

DOWN
1 King who signed the Magna Carta
2 Traveler ___ Polo
3 Armor material
4 The most famous Earp brother
5 It used to be the ninth planet
6 "Perfect!"
8 Haul away a wrecked car
9 Message ___ bottle (2 words)
10 Word ending after arch or trick
11 Spelling competition
12 Freshly painted
13 Sip a soda with this
14 Additional
15 Native American group
16 Squabble
17 Live and breathe
18 House for an old woman in a nursery rhyme

ACROSS

1 Computer clickers
3 Cupid's beloved
8 Largest land meat eater (2 words)
9 Largest marsupial (2 words)
15 One of the largest members of the cat family (2 words)
21 Largest animal on the planet (2 words)
22 Not present in school
23 White dwarf or red giant

DOWN

1 Lawn cutting machine
2 Like Superman or Batman
4 Show indifference
5 Cloudless
6 Hearing body part
7 Dog biter
10 Female sheep
11 Large barrel
12 Super Bowl organization: Abbr.
13 Princess Jasmine's prince
14 Third of three
16 Adjectives modify them
17 Dam that formed Lake Nasser
18 Mouse catcher
19 ___ White Shark
20 The Potomac is one
21 ___ constrictor (large snake)

ACROSS

1 Halloween prank ammunition (2 words)
4 ___ juice (camp drink)
6 Yellow pages listings
8 Vampires can't see themselves in one
9 Classic Walt Kelly comic strip
10 Half of MXXII
11 Response to a pinprick
13 Just say no
15 Cringe
16 Fly all alone
17 Nevada Museum of Art city
19 Confederate general's initials
20 News brief
21 Website log-on requirement
22 Droop
23 Tibetan ox
24 Girl in the family

DOWN

1 Juliet's betrothed in a Shakespeare play
2 Find them crawling in the soil
3 Find them crawling in the flower beds (2 words)
5 Like a sundae topping
7 Fly traps in the attic
12 Alien spaceship
14 Enjoyable
16 Like a snail trail
18 What big brothers are

· GOING WEST ·

ACROSS

1 Glass that splits light into the spectrum

4 Flowers that are red, but not blue

7 Way to get steers from the ranch to market in the old west (2 words)

8 Means by which pioneer families moved out west (2 words)

14 Method of horse-drawn travel in the old west

20 How the mail was delivered in the old west (2 words)

22 Sticky pine product

23 Sister's private journal

DOWN

1 Man of video games

2 Dog collar attachment

3 Juicy fruit

4 Air traffic control device

5 Kind of movies with aliens and spaceships

6 Winter toy

9 TV commercials

10 ___ diet (eating less)

11 Gift for Dad

12 "Long ___ in a galaxy far far away . . ."

13 CBS rival

15 Where Boy Scouts sleep

16 Shrek's color

17 Valentine's Day figure

18 Circus site

19 Part of a cowboy's boot

21 Scheming

· IT'S A TREAT ·

ACROSS

1 One way to describe 22 Across
3 Flying object
8 Ingredient in 22 Across
9 Ingredient in 22 Across
15 Performance genre for Alvin Ailey (2 words)
21 Places to make and eat 22 Across
22 Graham cracker treats with 8 Across and 9 Across
23 Use a keyboard

DOWN

1 German fairy tale brothers
2 Movie award
4 Hawaiian greeting
5 Move like a spider
6 Ham sandwich bread
7 Night-flying insect
10 Long ___ (in the past)
11 Observe
12 Homo sapiens
13 Hawaii's Mauna ___
14 Hobbit's enemy
16 Disney's flying elephant
17 Davy Crockett's Old Betsy
18 Sunless
19 Wicked
20 Spooky
21 PC data sources

ACROSS

1 Lose one's cool
4 Like old bread
7 Declaration of Independence signer from Massachusetts (2 words)
9 Declaration of Independence signer Francis ___ from New Jersey
14 Declaration of Independence signer Thomas ___ from Virginia
19 Declaration of Independence signer from Massachusetts (2 words)
21 Color of money
22 Smells awful

DOWN

1 Kindergarten stickum

2 Minor mythological deity
3 Sleazebucket
4 Florida city nicknamed "Gateway of the Americas"
5 Hawaii's Mauna ___
6 "You betcha!"
8 Night sky sight
10 Switch position
11 Prefix for plunk
12 "The Matrix" hero
13 Long sandwich
15 Patriot Allen of 1776
16 Mister, in Spanish
17 Nobody
18 Knee-slappers
19 Go for a run
20 Garden tool

	1		2		3		4			5		6

ACROSS

1 Dog drool
5 Playmate
7 Strawberry ___ cream
8 Seafood restaurant choice (3 words)
11 Grammy Awards category (3 words)
15 Easily decided (3 words)
20 Data from tree rings
21 Poorly lit
22 Dunce

DOWN

1 Soapy water
2 CB sign-off

3 Lunchbox fruit
4 Orange skin
5 South American country
6 Legal
9 Sci-fi transport
10 Driveway crack filler
11 Went on a rampage
12 Barbie's friend
13 Artful Dickens character
14 Wife of President Herbert Hoover
16 Netherlands cheese
17 Section of town
18 Honeybee's home
19 Tailless amphibian

SEASONAL SIGHTS
(PAGE 4)

WONDER FULL
(PAGE 5)

THANKSGIVING
(PAGE 6)

B	L	A	C	K		C	O	M	E	T
E		R		O		I				H
B	A	K	E	D	P	O	T	A	T	O
O			A		W		M			R
P	U	M	P	K	I	N	P	I	E	
	S		U		C		H		Y	
	A	P	P	L	E	C	I	D	E	R
C		I		A		O				O
R	O	A	S	T	T	U	R	K	E	Y
O		N		E		C		I		A
C	H	O	I	R		H	O	T	E	L

NOTED WOMEN
(PAGE 7)

IN GENERAL
(PAGE 8)

S	T	O	O	D		T	I	G	E	R
C		I		E		O		L		E
H	E	L	I	C	O	P	T	E	R	S
O		E		A		I		A		T
O	D	D	L	Y		C	O	M	M	A
L		I				F				U
G	A	M	E	S		A	F	T	E	R
I		U		O		W		H		A
R	E	S	E	R	V	A	T	I	O	N
L		I		T		K		N		T
S	A	C	K	S		E	D	G	E	S

GARDEN PATH
(PAGE 9)

S	A	L	A	D		S	P	I	N	E
N		A		A		A		O		G
I		S	U	N	F	L	O	W	E	R
F		E		C		E		A		E
F	O	R	G	E	T	M	E	N	O	T
	J		E		I		S		W	
H	O	N	E	Y	S	U	C	K	L	E
O		O		A		N		A		A
W	A	T	E	R	L	I	L	Y		T
L		E		D		T		A		I
S	O	D	A	S		Y	U	K	O	N

COLORING BOOK
(PAGE 10)

B	L	U	R	B		B	U	M	P	Y
I		P		U	S	A		U		E
T	A	P	I	R		N	A	S	A	L
T		E		N	B	A		I		L
E	G	R	E	T		N	A	C	H	O
R				O	N	A				W
S	E	W	E	R		M	Y	D	O	G
W		A		A	L	A		A		R
E	A	T	E	N		N	U	R	S	E
E		E		G	H	I		E		E
T	H	R	E	E		A	D	D	O	N

AROUND SCHOOL
(PAGE 11)

S	L	U	S	H		B	O	W	I	E
W		N		A		A		E		R
A		C	O	U	N	S	E	L	O	R
R		U		N		R		S		O
M	A	T	H	T	E	A	C	H	E	R
	L		A		G		H		C	
H	A	L	L	M	O	N	I	T	O	R
I		A		O		E		A		A
P	R	I	N	C	I	P	A	L		Z
P		R		K		A		K		O
O	A	S	I	S		L	A	Y	E	R

REAL STEEL
(PAGE 12)

FOUR FELINES
(PAGE 13)

STATE BIRDS
(PAGE 14)

IN THE KITCHEN
(PAGE 15)

BLUE-COLLAR JOBS
(PAGE 16)

WORD WEB 1
(PAGE 17)

TO-DO LIST
(PAGE 18)

ON THE MAP
(PAGE 19)

EAT YOUR VEGGIES
(PAGE 20)

BACK TO SCHOOL
(PAGE 21)

SPORTS FANS
(PAGE 22)

BUGGY
(PAGE 23)

WORD WEB 2
(PAGE 24)

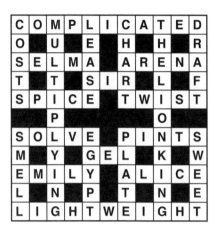

DINO DELIGHT
(PAGE 25)

ON THE CASE
(PAGE 26)

SCALE TAILS
(PAGE 27)

WHITE HOUSE
(PAGE 28)

G	R	A	N	T			T	Y	L	E	R
	L		I		W		E				
B	I	L	L	C	L	I	N	T	O	N	
A		O			S		T		N		
D	I	N	G	B	A	T		U	S	E	
	I		I		E			C			
B	I	G		G	A	D	G	E	T	S	
A		E		E			N			O	
H	A	R	R	Y	T	R	U	M	A	N	
	I		E		U		I				
A	D	A	M	S		N	I	X	O	N	

WATERLOGGED
(PAGE 29)

D	R	E	A	M			S	C	R	U	B
O		Y		A		H		A			I
G	R	E	E	N	L	A	N	D			L
	U		G		R		I			B
	M		H	O	K	K	A	I	D	O
	B		A		I		A			R
T	A	S	M	A	N	I	A			A
H		A		N		T			M
I		M	A	N	H	A	T	T	A	N
N		O		O		L		O		A
G	R	A	V	Y		Y	U	M	M	Y

FOUR SEASONS
(PAGE 30)

U	S	H	E	R			R	I	D	G	E
S		O		E		O		C		G	
E		H	O	T	S	P	R	I	N	G	
R		U		I		E		I			
S	U	M	M	E	R	S	T	O	C	K	
	T		A		U		E		H		
W	I	N	T	E	R	G	A	M	E	S	
	C		A		R		O		O		
W	A	T	E	R	F	A	L	L		U	
E		A		L		V		A		P	
B	A	G	G	Y		Y	A	R	D	S	

SICK DAYS
(PAGE 31)

B	A	R	K			S	N	E	E	Z	E
U		A				O		A		V	
S	C	H	O	O	L	N	U	R	S	E	
	H		N		A			T		N	
M	I	N	I		Y		C	H	A	T	
	N		O	L	D	E	R		U		
F	A	W	N		O		U	N	D	O	
E		A			W		S		I		
V	A	C	C	I	N	A	T	I	O	N	
E		K		C				L		U	
R	H	Y	M	E	S		F	L	A	T	

FAIRY TALES
(PAGE 32)

MUSIC MAKERS
(PAGE 33)

BORROWED
(PAGE 34)

EARLY START
(PAGE 35)

HIGH TECH
(PAGE 36)

V	I	R	U	S			S	I	M	O	N
I		O		E		O		I		O	
C		D	O	W	N	L	O	A	D	S	
E		N		I		M		M		I	
	F	L	A	S	H	D	R	I	V	E	
A		I		O		H		R		R	
S	M	A	R	T	P	H	O	N	E		
I		U		U		N				W	
D	V	D	P	L	A	Y	E	R		O	
E		I		I		A		E		R	
S	C	O	O	P		M	O	D	E	M	

LOOKING UP
(PAGE 37)

R	I	N	G	S		H	I	N	D	U
U		E		A		Y		O		S
D	O	W	N	T	O	E	A	R	T	H
E		B		I		N				E
	M	O	O	N	W	A	L	K	E	R
U		R		H			E			S
S	U	N	F	L	O	W	E	R	S	
E			A		A		A		A	
F	A	L	L	I	N	G	S	T	A	R
U		A		R		O		I		E
L	A	W	N	S		N	I	N	J	A

SHIVER ME TIMBERS
(PAGE 38)

R	O	C	K	Y		B	A	C	O	N
E		A		E		O		O		I
C	A	P	T	A	I	N	H	O	O	K
I		S		E		K		E		E
P	I	R	A	T	E	S	H	I	P	
E		I		L		N		N		G
	J	O	L	L	Y	R	O	G	E	R
A		T		O		A				A
T	R	E	A	S	U	R	E	M	A	P
O		R		E		E		O		E
M	A	S	T	S		R	O	O	T	S

WHAT'S FOR DINNER
(PAGE 39)

C	O	M	I	C		F	E	M	U	R
A		E		O		I		O		U
F	R	E	N	C	H	F	R	I	E	S
E		T		O		T		S		S
		S	P	A	G	H	E	T	T	I
S		A		O		G				A
C	H	I	L	I	D	O	G	S		
U		T		N		I		W		A
F	I	S	H	F	I	L	L	E	T	S
F		M		O		E		A		K
S	P	E	A	R		D	A	R	T	S

I WONDER
(PAGE 40)

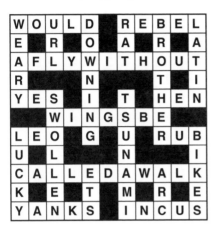

ZOO STORY
(PAGE 41)

UNDER THE BIG TOP
(PAGE 42)

READING MATERIAL
(PAGE 43)

JUST THE FACTS
(PAGE 44)

S	P	E	L	L	I	N	G	B	E	E
U		I		I		O		U		L
P	U	F	F	S		U	N	T	I	E
E		F		T	O	N		T		C
R	E	E	D	S		S	W	E	E	T
		L						R		
T	U	T	O	R		D	A	F	F	Y
U		O		E	C	O		L		A
L	O	W	E	R		U	N	I	O	N
I		E		U		G		E		K
P	A	R	E	N	T	H	E	S	E	S

GREAT BOOKS
(PAGE 45)

S	W	A	R	M		G	U	S	T	S		S
K		R		A		I		P		P	
Y		T	O	M	S	A	W	Y	E	R	
	A			I		N		R		A
O	L	I	V	E	R	T	W	I	S	T
	L		E		Y		H		L	
L	I	T	T	L	E	W	O	M	E	N
A		R		O		E			D	
T	H	E	H	O	B	B	I	T		T
E		A		N		E		E		O
R	A	T	T	Y			R	A	N	G	E

DON'T KNOCK IT
(PAGE 46)

N	E	G	E	V		P	R	I	M	P
I		A		O		H		N		O
L	I	G	H	T	S	O	C	K	E	T
E				E		T				A
	G	O	L	D	L	O	C	K	E	T
T		R		I			O			O
R	O	C	K	E	T	S	H	I	P	
O			N		E					W
P	O	C	K	E	T	W	A	T	C	H
H		A		M		E		R		E
Y	U	M	M	Y		R	H	Y	M	E

BIKINI BOTTOM
(PAGE 47)

H	U	M	P	S		I	N	T	W	O
I		E		L		R		A		D
J	E	L	L	Y	F	I	S	H		O
		O		L		S		O		R
S	A	N	D	Y	C	H	E	E	K	S
	I		A		R		R		I	
K	R	A	B	B	Y	P	A	T	T	Y
N		E		R		E		I		
E		S	Q	U	I	D	W	A	R	D
A		O		S		A		R		R
D	E	P	T	H		L	E	A	K	Y

THINGS THAT FLY
(PAGE 48)

MATH PROBLEMS
(PAGE 49)

CAREER DAY
(PAGE 50)

MY HERO
(PAGE 51)

FOR BREAKFAST
(PAGE 52)

ON TV
(PAGE 53)

WELL STATED
(PAGE 54)

PUPPY LOVE
(PAGE 55)

JUST DESSERTS
(PAGE 56)

CLEAN UP
(PAGE 57)

WORD WEB 3
(PAGE 58)

WIZ KIDS
(PAGE 59)

```
R O D E O S   G A L A
O   L   I   A     E
G U N F I G H T E R S
E   I   H   O   O
R E X   S T I R R U P
    O   C   Q   A
B A N D I T S   N A P
I     R   E   G   O
P O N Y E X P R E S S
E   E   A   E   S
D E E R   S A D D L E
```

```
B A S I C   F L A R E
A   I   O   R   R   M
H A R D D R I V E   A
  T   E   A   N   I
S E R V I C E C A L L
  U   I   E   U   O
A P P L I C A T I O N
P   A   A   I   S
P   R E P R I N T E D
L   T   O   A   H   Y
E G Y P T   M O U S E
```

```
B A T H S   M O C H A
O   A   A   U   O   S
W O R L D G L O B E S
L     A   C   R   I
  S K E T C H P A D S
S     S   A   O   T
C A L C U L A T O R
A   I   P   C   I
M I C R O S C O P E S
P   K   N   R   I   L
S A S H A   A N G L E
```

```
A S T R O   R O B I N
L   I   N   O   E   E
F I N D I N G N E M O
R   T   O   E   E
E   I G N O R E   N
D O N     N     R U B
  U   I C E A G E   E
  C   H   N   W   A
T H E L I O N K I N G
A   R   N   I   N   L
T I A N A   E D D I E
```

PARTY TIME
(PAGE 64)

WEATHER REPORT
(PAGE 65)

SEE THE USA
(PAGE 66)

DATE LINES
(PAGE 67)

JUST FOR FUN
(PAGE 68)

C	A	D	E	T		F	I	S	H	Y
U		R		W		A		O		E
B	R	O	K	E	N	B	O	N	E	S
E		O		E		L			T	
S		L	I	T	T	E	R	B	O	X
	W		D		E		E		N	
P	O	I	S	O	N	I	V	Y		V
	R		I		S		U		I	
S	M	E	L	L	Y	S	O	C	K	S
O		E		E		U		K		I
S	O	L	I	D		E	G	Y	P	T

TOP DOGS
(PAGE 69)

B	A	R	K		P	L	A	N	E	T
L		O		M		A		E		E
U		C	H	I	H	U	A	H	U	A
R		K		C		G		R		
B	A	S	S	E	T	H	O	U	N	D
	I		O		B		P		N	
I	R	I	S	H	S	E	T	T	E	R
	D		A		X		E		E	
G	R	E	A	T	D	A	N	E		N
U		A		E		M		T		E
M	E	L	O	D	Y		C	H	O	W

GIFT GIVING
(PAGE 70)

C	L	O	U	D		C	H	A	L	K
O		I		W		A		L		I
S	I	L	V	E	R	C	H	A	I	N
T			E		H		M		D	
	B	A	R	B	I	E	D	O	L	L
G		U		M		D		D		Y
L	I	G	H	T	S	A	B	E	R	
O		U		A		T			S	
B	A	S	E	B	A	L	L	B	A	T
E		T		B		A		U		A
S	C	A	R	Y		S	U	G	A	R

SMELLS AWFUL
(PAGE 71)

J	U	M	P	S		W	I	P	E	S
O		A		T		Y		L		W
H	O	R	S	E	M	A	N	U	R	E
N		C		E		T		T		L
	T	O	I	L	E	T	B	O	W	L
	O		N		R		E		E	
S	W	E	A	T	Y	F	E	E	T	
T		X		R		I		X		S
R	O	T	T	I	N	G	F	I	S	H
A		R		B		H		S		O
W	H	A	L	E		T	I	T	L	E

BIG BEASTS
(PAGE 72)

M	I	C	E		P	S	Y	C	H	E
O		A		F	H		L			A
W		P	O	L	A	R	B	E	A	R
E		E		E		U		A		
R	E	D	K	A	N	G	A	R	O	O
	W		E		F		L			N
B	E	N	G	A	L	T	I	G	E	R
	O		S		R		R			I
B	L	U	E	W	H	A	L	E		V
O		N		A		P		A		E
A	B	S	E	N	T		S	T	A	R

CREEPY-CRAWLY
(PAGE 73)

R	A	W	E	G	G			B	U	G
O			A		A	D	S			O
M	I	R	R	O	R		P	O	G	O
E		T		D	X	I				E
O	U	C	H		E		D	E	F	Y
	F		W	I	N	C	E		U	
S	O	L	O		S		R	E	N	O
L		R	E	L		W			L	
I	T	E	M		U	S	E	R	I	D
M			S	A	G		B		E	
Y	A	K				S	I	S	T	E	R

GOING WEST
(PAGE 74)

P	R	I	S	M		R	O	S	E	S
A		D		E		A		C		L
C	A	T	T	L	E	D	R	I	V	E
		A		O		A		F		D
W	A	G	O	N	T	R	A	I	N	
	D		N		I		G		B	
	S	T	A	G	E	C	O	A	C	H
S		E		R		U		R		
P	O	N	Y	E	X	P	R	E	S	S
U		T		E		I		N		L
R	E	S	I	N		D	I	A	R	Y

IT'S A TREAT
(PAGE 75)

G	O	O	P		S	A	U	C	E	R
R		S		M		L		R		Y
I		C	H	O	C	O	L	A	T	E
M		A		T		H		W		
M	A	R	S	H	M	A	L	L	O	W
	G		E		A		O		R	
M	O	D	E	R	N	D	A	N	C	E
		U		I		A		A		E
C	A	M	P	F	I	R	E	S		R
D		B		L		K		T		I
S	M	O	R	E	S		T	Y	P	E

OUR FOUNDERS
(PAGE 76)

P	A	N	I	C		M	O	L	D	Y
A		Y		R		I		O		E
S	A	M	U	E	L	A	D	A	M	S
T		P		E		M			O	
E		H	O	P	K	I	N	S	O	N
	H		F			E			N	
J	E	F	F	E	R	S	O	N		J
	R			T		E		O		O
J	O	H	N	H	A	N	C	O	C	K
O		O		A		O		N		E
G	R	E	E	N		R	E	E	K	S

TWO BY THREE
(PAGE 77)

S	L	O	B	B	E	R		P	A	L
U		V		A		I	C	E		A
D	E	N		N		R				W
S	U	R	F	A	N	D	T	U	R	F
	F		N			A				U
R	O	C	K	A	N	D	R	O	L	L
I		E			O			O		O
O	P	E	N	A	N	D	S	H	U	T
T		D		R		G		I		O
E		A	G	E		E		V		A
D	I	M		A	I	R	H	E	A	D